Musings of an Online Bookseller

by

JOHN LANDAHL

Peverell Press

Peverell Press
an imprint of *InfoStrategist.com*
Seattle, WA

ISBN 978-1-59243-332-2

Library of Congress Control No: 2011910768

Published June 30, 2011

TABLE OF CONTENTS

CHAPTER 1

Introduction

For Whom Is This Book Intended?

Although this book contains some information that will be helpful for new online booksellers, it's aimed primarily at old hands in this area of endeavor, especially those who already make extensive use of online forums. As a consequence, it isn't oriented towards getting started in online bookselling and contains only general information about the basics of the business. For more basic information the reader is referred to several books by other authors that I've found to be good starting points for online bookselling.

And it's oriented primarily toward online bookselling on Amazon.com, affectionately referred to among booksellers as "the Big River" or sometimes just "the River."

About This Book

As I've written I've found it difficult to organize the material in this book, hence the title *Musings of an Online Bookseller*. The online bookselling business is a complex one, which is no doubt part of its appeal for some. It's also a continually changing one, so one of the primary themes running through this book is that of change – change both in world of online bookselling and in the larger world that encompasses it. This change is in demographics, technology, and business practices. As you may notice, I started this book in 2007. Its completion was delayed by the bursting of the subprime mortgage bubble and the subsequent severe recession, which impacted my online bookselling business just as it did many other businesses.

The Appeal of Rafting the Big River

> "Amazon gets a lot of traffic." – longtime bookseller

Although there are numerous other venues for online bookselling, some of which I'll touch on later, the main reason this book is primarily concerned with Amazon Marketplace is the one stated so succinctly in the quotation above – Amazon enjoys immense and sustained popularity as a sales channel!

A secondary reason is that Amazon.com has some unique aspects as an online bookselling venue, the first of which is that it inspires such great customer loyalty that people often forget that there are other places to buy books online, something I'll term "Amazon myopia." There's also an intriguing phenomenon I'll call "Amazon confusion" in which customers often confuse buying from an Amazon Marketplace seller with buying direct from Amazon as a corporation. Amazon also has an unusually active and particularly interesting electronic forum system for its Marketplace sellers. I touch briefly on these topics below and elaborate on them later on in this book.

Amazon Market Dominance

I'll go into this topic in greater detail later on; suffice it to say at this point that many online booksellers report that their sales in Amazon Marketplace far outpace those through competing channels.

Amazon and Customer Loyalty

> "What I like about Amazon.com is you can search for 'P. D. James large print.'" – Nancy Landahl, Amazon customer

One key aspect of Amazon's extraordinary and sustained success is inspiring intense customer loyalty. By capitalizing on Internet search technology and focusing on creating a great customer experience, Amazon.com has been unusually successful in building customer loyalty over the past decade and a half.

Amazon Myopia

> "Some people don't know there's any place to buy books but Amazon." – established antiquarian book dealer

As the quotation above indicates, Amazon.com's popularity is such that many online book purchasers look no further than the listings on Amazon's website, a phenomenon I've termed "Amazon myopia." I've actually fallen into this category at times myself, as recently when it didn't even occur to me to look for a used copy of a popular book by Bernie Siegel elsewhere once I found copies in Amazon Marketplace starting at $0.55!

Amazon Confusion

> "Very prompt processing, price very competitive, I have always enjoyed shopping with Amazon, I have never experienced any problems with receiving nor ordering. I hope to continue doing business with Amazon as they are my first choice in Internet shopping." – an entry from a Marketplace seller's feedback

Here's a clear case where a customer didn't seem to understand that she was purchasing a book from a third-party seller rather than directly from Amazon.com itself. Another way of describing "Amazon confusion" is that apparently many customers don't differentiate between Amazon's partner sellers and Amazon.com as a corporation.

Because of this all-too-frequent confusion about whom customers are actually buying books from when they shop on Amazon, my experience is that it's difficult to build brand loyalty as an Amazon Marketplace seller. Although there are undoubtedly some exceptions, probably few Marketplace booksellers get a lot of repeat business or build up a clientele of customers. For most sellers, their clientele is Amazon's clientele. A corollary of this is that customers' perceptions of Amazon, positive or negative, carry over to its partner sellers, and vice versa.

Amazon Seller Forums

Amazon has created a system of electronic forums or bulletin boards for its sellers, something that's by no means unique to it as an online bookselling sales channel. What does differentiate it from other sales channels, though, is the number of frequent readers of and active contributors to these forums – certainly in the hundreds and very likely in the thousands, possibly even the tens of thousands. Like the other topics listed above, these forums will be discussed in greater detail later on.

CHAPTER 2

The Challenge: A Complex Business in a Changing World

The online bookselling business is a complex one operating against a backdrop of constant, even accelerating, technological change in addition to economic and demographic change. Some of the most important technology-driven economic shifts have been discussed in detail by Thomas Friedman in his bestselling book *The World Is Flat: A Brief History of the Twenty-First Century* and by Chris Anderson in his influential one *The Long Tail: Why the Future of Business Is Selling Less of More.* Some particularly important changes are summarized briefly below, illustrated with examples relevant to online bookselling, and discussed at greater length later on.

An Example of Change – Consolidation in the Used Bookselling Business

In his highly-regarded 2001 business book *The Long Tail: Why the Future of Business Is Selling Less of More,* Chris Anderson discusses the emergence of the online bookselling business over the past decade as one example of the "Long Tail," significant cumulative sales of large numbers of low-volume items, in action. He sets this example in the context of retailing and the Sears

Roebuck catalog when it was first issued over a century ago.

Backdrop: The Baby Boomers Retire

In the context of the U.S. and a number of other developed countries, we have the important demographic factor of the "baby boom" generation now starting to reach retirement age. The baby boom is defined as running from 1946 to 1964, so this period of a swelling retired population will last for a decade and a half.

Backdrop: "Flat World" Economic Shifts

In his influential 2005 book *The World Is Flat: A Brief History of the Twenty-First Century*, Thomas Friedman talks about some dramatic recent economic shifts he's noted, including outsourcing and what he terms "home sourcing".

Online Bookselling: A Prime Example of a "Flat World" Economic Shift

As just mentioned, in *The World is Flat: A Brief History of the Twenty-First Century* Friedman discusses an economic shift he terms "homesourcing" – the outsourcing of certain types of work to people who operate out of their homes rather than stores or offices, a product of the technological advancement that has emerged within the last decade. A prime example of homesourcing is the online bookselling business, which represents a major change in used book retailing, with a preponderance of sellers operating home-based bookstores.

Backdrop: Moore's Law

Not discussed by Thomas Friedman in *The World Is Flat: A Brief History of the Twenty-First Century* is the technological principle called Moore's Law, an empirical rule concerning ongoing rapid and dramatic improvement in semiconductor technology, i.e., computer chips, over the last 30 years which basically forecasts that we will continue to see substantial changes in digital technology and steeply declining prices for some time to come.

Barcode Scanners: An Example of Moore's Law

Small handheld barcode scanners and their associated cell phones or PDAs are an example of the operation of Moore's Law. They're new enough on the scene that they're not even mentioned in Steven Windwalker's otherwise comprehensive 2002 book on online bookselling. Current barcode scanner models are more compact and less expensive than older ones, and the cell phones and PDAs needed to operate them have also gotten less expensive, more powerful, and more sophisticated. One recent development is Bluetooth wireless connectivity for portable and handheld devices, making it possible to purchase a barcode scanner that can be physically separate from a cell phone or PDA, and therefore less conspicuous to use.

CHAPTER 3

The Larger Setting in Greater Depth

As discussed briefly above, the online bookselling business operates within a larger setting of global ecommerce and the "flat world" of Thomas Friedman, technological advancement forecast by Moore's Law, and demographic change, particularly the impending retirement of the baby boomer generation in the U.S.

My crystal ball is too murky to embolden me to make predictions as to how changes in these areas will affect the online bookselling business, so I'll limit myself to describing some foreseeable changes and sketching out some scenarios with regard to their impacts.

The Flat World of Thomas Friedman Elaborated

> "Change is hardest on those caught by surprise." – David Schlesinger as quoted by Friedman

I recently reread *The World Is Flat: A Brief History of the Twenty-First Century* and here summarize some of my observations about it relevant to the online bookselling business. To begin with, what, exactly, does Friedman mean by "The World Is Flat?" On one level, he's contrasting the familiar geography of Planet Earth with a different image, where travel time is eliminated as an economic consideration.

Here he's talking about what people usually express as "the world is shrinking," referring, for example, to live TV coverage in the U.S. of distant events like the 2004 tsunami in East Asia. He uses the image of a shrinking world in discussing what he classifies as three eras of globalization, in which over a period of centuries the world first goes from large to small and then suddenly to tiny.

On a different level, he's talking about a level economic playing field in which parts of India and China in particular can provide remote services like call centers and compete with the domestic U.S. and Japanese workforces. These services include routine tasks in accounting and research (p. 13). They also include software development. It's predictable that they will expand to include more sophisticated tasks, including technological innovation.

What's Suddenly Made the World Tiny? Fiber-Optics!

The "flat world" so intriguingly documented by Thomas Friedman is one characterized by ubiquitous, high-speed data communications. Friedman's key argument (p. 66), and one that I remembered from my first reading of his book, is that the Internet stock boom "... sparked a huge overinvestment in fiber-optic cable companies, which then laid massive amounts of fiber-optic cable on land and under the oceans, which dramatically drove down the cost of making a phone call or transmitting data anywhere in the world." And once in place, the capacity of a fiber-optic cable can be increased periodically by upgrading the transmission equipment at its ends as technology improves.

One point I'd overlooked on my first reading, though, is that this shrinking of distance and leveling of the economic playing field also applies to domestic employment. The key example here is "homesourcing," in which the airline JetBlue hires reservation agents in the Salt Lake City area who work at home but attend 4 hours a month of training at company facilities.

Although these agents can't be literally "anywhere" in the U.S., they can be scattered over a pretty large part of Utah, and when a customer calls one of them, they have no idea that the person they're talking to isn't sitting in a cubicle in a city office building. I'd been aware of jobs like this, for example, home-based telephone translators for foreign-language conversations, but I hadn't thought about them in the context of Friedman's book. Online bookselling, of course, is an example of a home-based business enterprise for those of us not fortunate enough or perhaps not even desiring to own a bricks-and-mortar bookstore.

Friedman is also talking about flattening in other senses, though, especially in terms of organizational hierarchies (p. 45). One example that impresses him is that of a solitary blogger who can not only duplicate the print journalism functions of writing articles but also the news network functions of audio interviews and pictures, and who attracts a wide readership. While it's not clear that this blogger is engaged in a profit-making business rather than simply pursuing an interesting hobby, the parallel with a solo online bookseller duplicating the functions of a traditional bookstore is clear.

International Shipping Improvements

> "My book was shipped the same day I place the order (I saw in the envelope), and I received it in 3 labor days (I live in Spain, the seller in U.S.A.). I was gladly surprised . . ." – my own feedback on 3/5/07 (I got 5 stars from this satisfied buyer!)

Another aspect of the "flat world" not discussed by Friedman is increased ease of international shipping of books due to changes by the U.S. Postal Service a couple of years ago. As this feedback shows, packages can get to international buyers very quickly, in some cases even faster than to domestic ones who elect standard shipping by Media Mail.

The Inevitability of Change

Friedman quotes a particularly good summary from another author (David Schlesinger, who was at the time the head of Reuters America) of the inevitability of economic and technological change which includes the following assertions, already mentioned earlier:

> "Change is hard. Change is hardest on those caught by surprise. Change is hardest on those who have difficulty changing too. But change is natural; change is not new; change is important."

Interestingly, though, nowhere does Friedman mention Moore's Law, a major driving force behind technological change (see below).

The Implications of Moore's Law

The operation of Moore's Law (actually, despite its name, an observation or empirical rule rather than a natural law) concerning ongoing rapid and dramatic improvement in computer chips has arguably been the driving force in global technological innovation for the past several decades. First articulated by then-IBM and later Intel executive Gordon Moore in 1980, Moore's Law can be summarized as "The semiconductor industry doubles the price/performance [ratio] of its products roughly every 18 months" due to advances in microminiaturization technology. Not surprisingly, Bill Gates provides a well-informed discussion of Moore's Law in his 1995 book *The Road Ahead.*

Perhaps one of the most familiar examples of the operation of Moore's Law in recent years has been the increase in storage capacity and the fall of price for extra memory cards for digital cameras and cell phones. Without going into detail on this, if you own a digital camera you've probably noticed that over the years the memory cards available for it have gone from 16MB to 256MB to 512MB to 1 GB to 2GB and today even to 4GB or 8GB without getting physically larger (for example, a 4GB Compact Flash card fits into the same slot as a 16MB one) and that the price for an individual card is seldom more and sometimes less than that of it lower-capacity predecessor. The same has been true for USB thumb drives for personal computers.

You may have also noticed that newer types of memory cards are not just cheaper but also physically much smaller than older types – the newer ones are more like a postage stamp than a credit card or a match book, as in the past. Cell phones are a particularly familiar example of digital electronic devices which have gotten noticeably smaller over the past decade as well.

Note that, strictly speaking, Moore's Law applies only to semiconductors, not to hard drives, removable storage media like floppy disks, CDs, and DVDs, or to batteries. Even so, technological innovation has increased the capacity and/or reduced the size and price of these also. One obvious place where Moore's Law has impacted the online bookselling business is by making possible the development of handheld barcode scanners for ISBNs (see below).

How Long Will Moore's Law Hold?

Moore's Law was never postulated as holding indefinitely. Ultimately semiconductor microminiaturization will come up against limits set by the dimensions of individual atoms or other physical limitations. When will this occur? Probably not for roughly another decade, and even when it does, innovation will continue in materials and design.

What does this technological progress mean? Among other things, that the size of handheld electronic devices will continue to shrink, their speed and capacity will continue to increase, and their prices will continue to fall for years to come. In terms of the online bookselling business, the prediction here is that handheld scanners will become both more sophisticated and more affordable with the passage of time.

Outside the Scope of Moore's Law

In the world of computers, the emergence of the Internet was unforeseen at the time Moore's Law was first postulated. It was not specifically a product of microminiaturization, and it's telling that even Microsoft, which was watching with not unwarranted paranoia for the arising of disruptive new technologies that would impact its business, recognized its emergence only when it was almost too late to reorient its business to capitalize on the opportunities it provides.

Fiber-Optic Technology and the Future

In his 1995 book *Being Digital*, Nicholas Negroponte, Director of MIT's Media Lab, noted that "we literally do not know how many bits per second we can send down a fiber." A few years later, an article in the Jan. 20, 2000, issue of *The Wall Street Journal* summarized some of the reasons for this. According to this article, ". . . the amount of information that can be transmitted over a strand of glass is doubling every nine to 12 months."

Fiber-optic technology basically involves using lasers to send pulses of light through a glass fiber. The speed of light being a constant (roughly one foot per nanosecond, a nanosecond being one billionth of a second), advances in fiber-optic technology enumerated in the article fall into three basic categories – increasing the number of pulses transmitted in a given time, transmitting additional streams of pulses through the same glass fiber simultaneously, and reducing attenuation of the signals as they travel along the fiber. The article reports that a single fiber-optic beam could carry 2.5 megabits of digital information per second in 1996, and that increasing the number of pulses had increased this capacity to 10 megabits per second by 2000.

Additional streams of pulses can be transmitted by sending them using light beams of different colors, taking advantage of the fact that light beams do not interfere with one another. According to the article, commercial systems using 16 colors per fiber were introduced in 1996, and new commercial systems available in 2000 used 80 colors. Experimental systems using 1,022 colors were already being tested in the laboratory by then.

Thus a fiber-optic cable installed in 1996 could be used to carry 20 times as much data in 2000 by upgrading its laser equipment, and could be projected to carry at least 200 times as much data within a few years. This potential for dramatically increasing the capacity of an existing cable is important because of the high labor cost typically involved with installing additional cable.

It was foreseeable at the time this article appeared that where this capacity increase would have its greatest initial impact was the long-distance lines of telecommunication companies, bringing about further reductions in already-falling long-distance telephone rates, for example. At the time I read it I misunderstood what was happening and thought this capacity increase would result in fiber-optic trunk lines within urban neighborhoods and that it would later manifest itself both in lower costs and in availability of higher bandwidth for Internet connectivity for businesses and homes.

That was because one key point that escaped me in all the excitement about the dot-com era "bandwidth tsunami" (as one investment firm labeled it) was that it didn't extend to "the last mile" (the final connection to the home) domestically because of provisions of the U.S. telecommunications deregulation acts. At the time I thought that the "bandwidth tsunami" would mean immediate low-cost broadband to the residence, but it really didn't, so the short-term impact on the consumer market was much less than I anticipated. It took years for affordable broadband to become available, and even today it's primarily restricted to urban areas.

Bottom line: Bandwidth will be increasing dramatically for some time to come, even if microprocessor technology plateaus and sales of desktop computers slow.

CHAPTER 4

In Greater Detail: Complexities of the Business

> "I still consider myself a new seller after almost a year of slowly building up." – Amazon seller forum contributor, 2007

Several excellent books about getting started in the online book business have been published in the last ten years, but even disregarding technological change, it seems that this is a business where no matter how much you know, there's always more to learn! Complexities of the business include selection and acquisition of inventory, pricing, choice of distribution channels, and shipment methods. This is even more the case because distribution channels, Amazon included, keep changing their systems and their rules!

The "Book Universe"

At the root of this business complexity is the inherent complexity of the "book universe." A large library or bookstore with in excess of 40,000 books divided into dozens of genres and subgenres (mystery, romance, literature, poetry, history, biography, reference, etc.) can be a bewildering place to wander through! Judging by the sales ranks of the slowest selling books, Amazon.com presently lists in excess of 10 million books, or 2500 times that many, and more books are being added daily! On closer examination, the number of books is clearly considerably overstated because many have duplicate product detail pages, but the number is nonetheless far greater than that to be found in any physical bookstore.

The Myriad of Editions: One Key Source of Complexity

One might justifiably argue that, in addition those that are outright duplicates, as just mentioned, many more of these 10 million or more Amazon.com listings are merely for different editions of the same book (hardcover, paperback, revised edition, etc.). However, since each of these editions can have a different value in the marketplace, we've not simplified matters but merely identified another source of business complexity.

A Note on Amazon Sales Ranks

Amazon sales ranks run from 1 for the best-selling item in a category to more than 10 million at this point for the worst-selling one in the "books" category. Though a natural enough way to rank books, this also creates a problem with terminology. That's because it's likewise natural to want to refer to a book that sells strongly as having a "high" sales rank, meaning at the top of the ladder of sales success. However, from a numerical standpoint a book with a high sales rank is actually one that sells slowly! One could, of course, say that a book that sells well has a "good" sales rank, but that's a little vague.

Pace of Change and Outdated Information

Useful as they are, the existing books on online bookselling unavoidably contain some outdated information, due to the rapid pace of change. Fortunately in many cases their authors frequently update this information in their blogs.

CHAPTER 5

The Amazon Seller Discussion Boards

A Vast Resource

> ". . . when I first started on Amazon, I read through each board for about 3-4 hours straight (over the course of a week, of course) – going back about 2 years on each . . ." – Amazon seller forum contributor, 2007

A tremendous resource for up-to-date information on all aspects of online bookselling is the Amazon seller discussion boards. These boards have their drawbacks as well as their advantages, however. While, as the above quotation indicates, these boards are a terrific place to get the most up-to-date information about almost any aspect of the online bookselling business, they're so voluminous and "noisy" (in the sense of including a large amount of repetitive and irrelevant information) that finding accurate, pertinent information can be a frustrating and time-consuming matter. I'll summarize the most relevant information about a few of the more frequently mentioned topics of discussion in later chapters. However, these boards are so important that I'll digress and discuss certain aspects of them in some detail at this point and mention suggested search strings to help you locate current discussions on particular topics.

Online Bookseller Culture on the Amazon Boards

The online bookseller culture revealed by discussions on the Amazon boards might on first acquaintance appear somewhat schizophrenic – a combination of genteel sociability and vocal paranoia. As one might expect, this in part reflects the fact that there are many friendly, sociable online booksellers and also a number of paranoid, reclusive ones. However, on closer examination, there are comprehensible reasons why even individual booksellers, no matter how inclined to be outgoing and helpful to their compatriots, are apt to seem paranoid from time to time.

An Example of Paranoia

An example of apparently excessive paranoia I encountered early on was a series of replies to an innocent newbie post on the Amazon Seller's Soapbox board entitled, "So, Where Y'all From?" A number of contributors responded congenially with specific information – Yuma, Arizona, for example. A few gave vague replies – "earth," "out there."

One said that he no longer revealed his location because he'd found it helped others to identify his sources for inventory and draw on them too – what an old-time gold prospector might term claim-jumping. Another said matter-of-factly that if he could figure out the location of another seller with a similar inventory within a 4-hour driving radius, he would definitely go there to search for sources of inventory.

An Exceptionally Forthcoming Online Bookseller

In contrast, on the last day (half-price day) of a large local Friends of the Library book sale, I saw a woman with a handheld scanner systematically scanning the barcodes of the books left in the "better books" section, where books were either priced individually at up to $5 or so or generically at twice the price in the main sales area. I heard someone asking her why she was bothering after dozens of other online booksellers had repeatedly scanned the same books during the previous two days of the sale. She replied quite cordially and forthrightly that she was happy making $5 on a book and that other sellers didn't like to ship that many. Evidently the 50% price drop on the final day of the sale brought enough books of the number remaining into her target profitability range to make it worthwhile for her to scan the rejects and purchase some.

She went further and explained how her scanner showed sales rank as well as price, apparently unconcerned that the fellow she was talking to would say,

"What a great idea!" and come back to the next sale with a shiny new scanner to do exactly the same thing. So obviously at least some online booksellers have an impulse to share information and interact with others who may then decide to embark energetically on the same line of endeavor.

It's an Explicable Paranoia

In contrast, many online booksellers feel that they have good reason for paranoia. Certainly one thing that comes to mind in this context is Intel executive Andrew Grove's 1996 book about the personal computer industry, *Only the Paranoid Survive.*

As I've written this book, I've personally found myself torn between revealing information and withholding it. At times I've felt that the concerns some Amazon Marketplace sellers voice about revealing "trade secrets" are exaggerated because the online bookselling business is so complex that there's room for plenty of different but successful strategies, and that it has so many uncertainties that many who try it will drop out when they discover it's not as easy a way to make money as they'd imagined.

On the other hand, barriers to entry to online bookselling are indeed low. I certainly see competitors with barcode scanners working the shelves from time to time in the thrift stores I frequent, and they congregate by the dozens or even the hundreds at the big used book sales. Naturally, my first reaction when I see someone doing this is that they're beating me to all the good books! However, I also realize that these days concealing information from those who remember that "Google is your friend" is difficult indeed!

Some Patterns in Responses to Forum Posts

> "The 'oldies' . . . have posted a ton of advice . . . about shipping, packaging, customer service, listing, and other helpful things." – Amazon forum contributor, 2008

A close look at the Amazon seller boards will reveal certain patterns of responses to comments and queries, especially those from newbies. Posts celebrating valuable finds and giving details of favorite sources of inventory usually trigger a flood of negative comments from experienced sellers, often expressing hostility and scorn in scathingly caustic language. On the other hand, posts asking for information about business mechanics – shipping, packaging, listing, etc. – usually receive immediate polite, helpful replies, often from these same experienced sellers.

Not a Support Group

> "These ARE competitors and not support groupies so with that in mind . . . Being in business for yourself is not the same as getting a new job at a company where the other workers welcome you in and get you a cup of coffee and help you out. Here you will get plenty of help, but remember you are basically on your own . . ." – Amazon forum contributor, 2008

The key point to understand here is that, as the preceding quote states, the Amazon seller boards are *not* a support group (eBay's bookseller board is usually much more of one, as discussed below). They're a forum for information exchange, but with some unwritten community rules. These rules are more readily understood when we consider where individual sellers' interests align and where they diverge.

Aligned and Divergent Interests

In aspects of the online bookselling business in which individual sellers' interests align, it's certainly to their benefit to cooperate and collaborate, and the Amazon discussion forums provide an excellent mechanism for doing this. Concerning aspects in which they diverge, some vocal forum contributors can always be counted on to respond abruptly, even rudely, to forum posts and to endeavor to discourage further discussion.

Divergent Interests

What are the sellers' interests that diverge? They're easy to identify – anything that falls in the area of direct competition. That includes price competition and competition for inventory. Part of the immediate and intense disapprobation that's the usual response to revealing sources of quality inventory is based on the fear of drawing more entrants to the business.

Boasting about a valuable find has an important and predictable effect on price competition because publicizing the item will naturally lead others to seek it out and list it, increasing the supply, which can cause its price to fall, sometimes dramatically. For example, in July, 2008, an Amazon newbie boasted about finding a scarce $100 VHS video set for $10 at the thrift store their first time out with a handheld barcode scanner. Experienced sellers immediately pointed out that since he gave the name of the set in his post several more copies would likely appear on Amazon within a few days, driving prices sharply down and reducing the value of this find considerably.

Aligned Interests

> 1 out of 5: "I WILL NEVER USE AMAZON.COM AGAIN AND I WANT MY MONEY BACK" – Amazon seller's feedback, May, 2008

> 1 out of 5: "VERY UNHAPPY CUSTOMER. I placed an order on 4/14/08 and it was stated the expected ship date as 4/16/08. Today is 5/10/08 and I still have not received my order. In the meantime I have had to purchase the book from another place (at full price). On 4/28/08 I sent an email to [the seller]. Still no response. Is this good business practice? It will be a long time before I use Amazon again." – another Amazon seller's feedback, May, 2008

Interests of online booksellers that are aligned are at first less obvious, but these quotes certainly pinpoint one area – customer satisfaction. I won't go into the issue of the validity of these two customers' complaints here – perhaps they have merit or possibly they're totally unwarranted or due to circumstances beyond a seller's control, like a serious illness. The point I want to illustrate is that, because of "Amazon confusion" (see above), dissatisfied customers evidently often take their experience with any Amazon Marketplace transaction as indicative of the marketplace as a whole rather than of an individual seller.

The more customers who swear off Amazon forever and in toto, the less the demand will be for the wares of each individual Marketplace seller. Thus online booksellers' interests are aligned in the area of order fulfillment and customer service, and these are the topics where experienced sellers are always happy to help others.

Using the Amazon Seller Boards Effectively

> "I read [these discussion boards] like a maniac – what fun! Soaked it all in . . ." – Amazon seller forum contributor, 2007

> ". . . I read these boards for weeks, hours and hours each day, going back years worth of posts, before I ever typed a word . . ." – Amazon forum contributor, 2008

There's certainly wisdom to this approach, even if you've long been a contributor to other forums. To reiterate, these particular boards aren't a support group and it's easy to post an innocent comment or question that will trigger a barrage of caustic replies. It's also polite to search the boards for a topic before posting a question, and likewise practical since certain questions are asked frequently by newbies (sometimes two or three times a week!) and will just get replies that say "see the earlier thread on this topic."

The Amazon boards do have "OT" (off-topic) threads where online booksellers socialize and philosophize, sometimes companionably and sometimes contentiously, but it's important to put "OT" at the beginning of the subject line to alert readers when a post is not directly related to online bookselling.

eBay's More Sociable Forum

The eBay bookseller forum seems more oriented toward sharing information congenially than the Amazon boards, where anyone who posts detailed information about sources of inventory is likely to be the recipient of numerous critical comments to the effect that "you're making life harder for the rest of us." The reasons for this difference between Amazon and eBay as sales channels are open to debate, but may have to do with the difference between selling goods at auction vs. at fixed price or between the culture of openness and community long promoted by eBay and the much different culture that has evolved on its own on the Amazon boards.

As an example, on the Amazon boards it's regarded as patently self-destructive to post the names of books that have sold for particularly high prices in Amazon Marketplace, where there's no way to determine selling prices, only list prices. If a book's listing disappears, did it sell at the asking price or did the seller give up on it and cancel the listing? There's no way to tell.

The eBay boards, on the other hand, have a special thread for posting information about particularly valuable books. That's no secret on eBay because members can view recent completed listings to see prices – a feature I've drawn on in compiling the appendix to this book, *Some Ugly Ducklings Amongst Used Books, 2007*, in which I list 58 ordinary-appearing books that sold for more than $100 each on eBay in the latter part of 2007.

CHAPTER 6

Three Acknowledged Online Bookselling Authorities

Although at this point there are a number of books on online bookselling, three classics among them are the comprehensive guides by Steve Weber, Stephen Windwalker, and Michael Mould. In this book I refer primarily to those by Weber and Mould because they're the ones I'm most familiar with. I'll discuss each of these author's books in greater depth in the next chapter, but here I give a little background on the authors themselves so you'll have an idea of their perspectives, which are somewhat different.

Steve Weber, author of *The Home-Based Bookstore*

Steve Weber discovered the opportunities in selling books online on his own in 1998, starting with Half.com. He has a background in journalism which reveals itself in the clarity and organization of his writing.

Stephen Windwalker, author of *Selling Used Books Online*

I'd wondered about Stephen's surname "Windwalker" when I first heard about his book – turns out it reflects the fact he's a Cherokee Indian (as it happens I'm part Metlakatla, an Alaska Native tribe, myself). He was involved in the used bookselling business for over a decade before getting into online sales soon after the distribution channel began to appear, so he knows the inner workings of the bricks-and-mortar bookstore business well. He understands equally well the anxieties of small booksellers about competition from big business entities like Amazon.com, Barnes and Noble, etc., but also sees and elucidates the counterintuitive reasons for embracing Amazon.com as a business partner.

Michael Mould, author of *Online Bookselling*

A key point to keep in mind in reading Mould's book is that the author describes himself as having the goal of bringing in supplemental income without risking burnout by working overtime at his high-stress day job as a mechanical engineer at a major commercial airplane manufacturer. Although he describes one of his sons as bringing in as much as $10,000 a month selling books online, he also indicates that this level of success can't be attained in every major metropolitan area, and presumably it would be very difficult to achieve in a small town. His wife also helps him with some aspects of his business, so he's not working strictly solo.

CHAPTER 7

Particularly Useful Books for Beginners

In the previous chapter I listed three important authors in the field of online bookselling. Now I'll discuss each of their books in detail.

Online Bookselling by Michael Mould

I begin with *Online Bookselling* by Michael Mould because it serves to illustrate the theme of change that I reiterate so frequently throughout this book. The first edition of *Online Bookselling* was published in February of 2006 and the revised and updated edition was released in May of the same year. Since the revisions and updates appear to have been made primarily by adding footnotes, it's clear that even during this brief period Mould's advice has changed in response to changes in the bookselling distribution channels he utilizes.

In his chapter "Where to Sell Your Books" he devotes a long section to AbeBooks based on years of experience as a satisfied subscriber and describes in considerable detail its advantages as a distribution channel. However, in a paragraph on p. 77 he discusses some recent changes in its service that had just lowered it in his estimation, and in a footnote at the bottom of the same page he says he will soon be dropping his subscription. One reason he gives for this decision is that changes at Amazon.com have made international shipping easier, which was previously a major reason for selling through AbeBooks.

Mould's section on Alibris begins, "Alibris.com is my personal favorite listing service . . . there is nothing about this service that I do not like." However, in a footnote at the bottom of page 79 added a few months later, Mould says, "With their institution of the $0.25 charge for all Amazon orders processed through Alibris, some of what was appealing about the Alibris marketplace to me has been tarnished."

The point here is not the relative merits of AbeBooks, Alibris, and Amazon Marketplace as distribution channels – it's that the players in the industry are constantly changing their business practices as they jockey for market share and to maintain profitability, and these changes may not always be to the good from the standpoint of an online bookseller. Beyond this tactical jockeying, larger shifts are also occurring. For example, Mould reports that Alibris was acquired by a larger company (Oak Hill Capital Partners) in March, 2006, which could have something to do with the institution of that additional $0.25 charge that so changed his opinion of them!

An example of a recent change made by Amazon has been to offer the Amazon Mailing Service to simplify the process of purchasing postage and printing mailing labels for third-party Amazon sellers.

A Business Perspective

One important perspective on online bookselling is the traditional business viewpoint. By this I mean a conventional business plan analysis dealing with aspects such as competition, barriers to entry, initial capitalization, and cash flow. Michael Mould's book is strong in this area.

Personal Practices

How does Mould personally approach online bookselling? He says he does it part-time to bring in supplemental income and sometimes gets help from his wife. He goes on to say his favorite sources for inventory are local library fundraising shelves, which he makes a point of visiting frequently (several times a week) and bookstore clearance shelves, and that he generally pays between $0.25 and $3.00 per book. In addition he attends a variety of other kinds of sales.

He concentrates on books in particular categories he's found to yield a high percentage of valuable books and avoids those in certain other categories he's found to be generally disappointing in terms of value. Within his preferred categories he selects promising books and checks their value with a cellphone service that reports their sales rank and gives the prices of the three lowest-priced copies, since the cheapest copy may be a damaged one with an atypically low price. Interestingly, he says that he types in the ISBN rather than using a barcode scanner.

He sells his books through multiple online distribution channels and keeps careful track of sales transactions. His businesslike approach enables him to report that for his last 3000 sales, his average sales price was $6.95 per book, his average cost was $1.64, and his average profit was $5.31 (p. 29). He says he now keeps less careful track of his time, but at one point calculated that he was making $35 an hour (p. 20).

The Home-Based Bookstore by Steve Weber

This is an attractive book in terms of design, organization, and typography, and when I checked out a copy from my local library I wanted to start reading it right away! And when I saw Appendix 7, Glossary, with definitions of terms like "dog-earred" and "chipped" for describing used books, I decided to buy my own copy at once just to have that information to refer to!

Things that caught my attention on skimming quickly through it were that that the income potential was estimated to be $40,000 a year, that the place to focus is certain kinds of nonfiction rather than fiction, and that you can make money on $2-$3 books.

Although it's not compendious, this book is thorough and comprehensive in covering topics such as where to get used books (there are lots of places I hadn't thought of) and a full range of options for selling them online. It also includes information on Half.com, eBay Stores, and Amazon Auctions, sales channels I wasn't familiar with. One particularly clever and useful suggestion for minimizing startup costs was to start with books you already have. The description of Amazon Marketplace as a reverse auction in which sellers jockey to offer the lowest price gave me a much more insightful perspective on how that system works.

Steve also talks about the importance of using a SKU system for keeping track of inventory and gives an idea of how long to keep trying if a book doesn't sell – 18 months for books under $10 is his recommendation. He helpfully discusses a lot of problems that can arise in dealing with customers and gives advice about how to deal with them. He also discusses barcode scanning and Internet database technology for getting prices of books.

One thing that Steve points out is that books have a number of advantages, including standard descriptions, durability in shipping, and few problems with frauds for those selling for under $20. His book has plenty of other small but very useful insights and tidbits of information.

Selling Used Books Online by Stephen Windwalker

I personally found *Selling Used Books Online* absorbing, insightful, and illuminating. Recently some have criticized Windwalker's book as being outdated because it doesn't discuss topics like barcode scanners, but what it does cover it covers very well and in considerable depth.

One point I picked up on reading this book is the purpose of refreshing listings, which is to get them displayed early in the list of copies for sale. Contributors to the Amazon seller boards frequently advise closing listings and then reposting them in response to posts by novice sellers concerned about slumping sales, but I wasn't clear why this was recommended.

Elsewhere Steve describes his book as a labor of love and that shows in the writing. He's an avid bookseller who clearly set out to write a thoughtful, valuable book.

Which Online Bookselling Guide Should You Buy?

If you're an established online bookseller you probably already own at least one of these three books already. If you're just starting out, there's no single book that's so comprehensive and up-to-date that it's the only one you'll find useful. As you progress in online bookselling, you'll probably find it helpful to buy an additional book related to the subject from time to time because you'll undoubted pick up a few tips from it that you didn't get in other books, or perhaps that just didn't fully register the first time you encountered them.

CHAPTER 8

My Own Perspective

Rather than reiterating the information contained in the three comprehensive guides listed above, this book, as you'll have noticed, approaches online bookselling from a different perspective. I began by setting online bookselling in the larger framework of Thomas Friedman's "flat world" and the technological rule of thumb known somewhat misleadingly as Moore's Law (I say misleadingly because it's not a physical law like the Law of Gravitation). Now I'll give you a little of my own background.

My Own Online Bookselling History

I'll emphasize at this point that I still consider myself a relatively new Amazon Marketplace online bookseller, and a very small one at that. There's a reason why I'm so small – I don't have much storage space for inventory in my apartment, which means that to expand my stock I'd have to rent heated storage space.

Lack of opportunity to acquire inventory isn't an issue, since I live in a densely-populated urban area near several large thrift stores and with plenty of yard sales in the summertime in addition to estate sales year around. However, I'm up against plenty of competition from other bricks-and-mortar and online booksellers for quality inventory. If I go to an estate sale half an hour before it opens, I typically find at least four or five other dealers in line before me at the door, and sometimes several more surge in right behind me, head straight for the books, and set briskly to work with barcode scanners.

Although I'm a relative newcomer to Amazon Marketplace, I'm an experienced eBay seller, and I've even written a book about selling on eBay (*Estate Sale Prospecting with Craigslist and eBay*, 2006). While I do sell books on eBay, at this point I put most of my bookselling effort into Amazon Marketplace.

Amazon vs. eBay

If you've been selling books or other items on eBay and are starting to move into selling books in Amazon Marketplace, by all means search the Amazon seller forums for a thread about "Important Amazon Rules to Learn." This is a FAQ to help eBay sellers who are new to Amazon understand the differences between the two systems, some of which are very important not to overlook.

Unlike some other small online booksellers, I'm not a hobby seller – I'm definitely looking to make profitable sales, and plenty of them! As a result I pay careful attention to holding down my business expenses and getting a good return on my investment in inventory. In the early days of starting my business, I also worked with a small business counselor at the Seattle SCORE (Service Corps of Retired Executives) office who advised me on ways to improve my operation.

How I Operate Right Now

At this point I'm focusing on collectible books to get the best use out of my small available space for inventory storage. A couple of years ago I started to use a handheld barcode scanner. Prior to that, when I had the luxury of time to do so, I preferred to jot down the titles and ISBNs of books I found. Then I would go off to a nearby public library and check their values and sales ranks in Amazon Marketplace before deciding which ones to buy. Of course this wasn't always possible, and deferring purchases meant that sometimes someone else bought a book before I could make my decision and return for it.

I list books individually on Amazon, first typing a detailed description with a word processor, since that allows me to use larger type to accommodate my aging eyesight, and then pasting it into the Condition field.

I rarely price a book below the lowest priced one in the same condition, reasoning that if I do someone's automatic repricing software will undercut me in a day or two, and often price it a little on the high side, at least to start with. I don't cull my inventory very often because many of the books I select have very high Amazon sales ranks (above 3M) and can therefore take quite some time to sell. Because every now and then a book I've come to think will *never* sell finally does, I'm hesitant to give up even on books I've had listed for two years or longer.

I print my own electronic postage using Amazon's postage purchase option and always ship books using delivery confirmation (included in the postage price anyway) for the limited but useful tracking ability it provides (USPS insists that Delivery Confirmation is not a true tracking system, although it certainly comes close to one in some respects). For small, light items like music CDs ordered with standard shipping, I often give customers a courtesy upgrade to First Class Mail.

My Current Business Philosophy

> "I only started 3 1/2 years ago . . . All during this time, I was also navigating the learning curve of branching out to multiple venues and jumping over to online postage (and finally a thermal label printer). And most importantly I learned what it took to keep customers SATISFIED and am very proud of my 100% feedback . . . My advice to ANYONE trying out on-line selling is to start small and grow slow." – Amazon forum contributor, 2008

Although my initial impulse after reading Steve Weber's book was certainly to plunge energetically into online bookselling full-time, because of the complexities of the online bookselling business summarized in the introduction, I've adopted a more patient and cautious approach recognizing that I definitely have lessons to learn. Note this Amazon forum contributor says he or she "only started 3 1/2 years ago." In some areas of endeavor 3 1/2 years would be a long time, but not in the case of online bookselling!

CHAPTER 9

The Learning Curve

In the Introduction I discuss the complexity of the online bookselling business. A correlate of this complexity is a long learning curve. I'll illustrate the beginnings of the learning curve with my own experiences.

My Own Learning Curve

In mid-2006 I decided to try selling books online in Amazon Marketplace. I opened a basic seller account and over a period of a couple of months listed sixty books, some that I'd found at estate sales and some of my own that I wanted to get rid of.

Having no experience in selling on Amazon Marketplace, I approached it as I would selling on eBay, where I did have considerable experience. I picked books that I myself had read and liked, including a number my favorite mystery authors like P.D. James and Tony Hillerman. I didn't sell a single book, and when my listings started to expire after 60 days I didn't bother to relist them.

eBay Selling

For eBay, it can be a fairly successful strategy to pick popular vintage items like glass insulators to buy and resell. There are several reasons for this. One is that with popular items there will be a number listed at auction plus a number of recently completed sales, making it easy to set a price.

You'll also see within a week how the market responds to your listing, and if you price your item low to start with and offer inexpensive shipping, you have a good chance of selling it and clearing it out of your inventory. If it turns out that the supply is large relative to the demand, you may take a loss on it, but you can rationalize that you've learned something in the process.

Books in Amazon Marketplace Are Different

Books in Amazon Marketplace are different, but I didn't realize it at the time. The first time around, some books I never bothered to list at all because when I checked the prices I found that there were already lots of penny copies for sale. Other books I sold on eBay, where it looked to me like they might go for higher prices, but of course if they don't sell there you're out some money in the form of listing fees.

The net result of my experiences was that I wrote a rather pessimistic appendix about selling books in Amazon Marketplace in my 2006 book *Estate Sale Prospecting for Fun and Profit with craigslist and eBay.*

Finding a Most Helpful Book

After *Estate Sale Prospecting* went up for sale on Amazon.com, I noticed that some purchasers of it had also bought *The Home-Based Bookstore* by Steve Weber. (There's good reason for this. As Steve mentions in his blog review of my book on estate sale prospecting, he frequently goes to estate sales to buy books and likes the idea of picking up one or two other interesting things with potential resale value on eBay in the process.)

When I got a copy of his book and started reading it, I found out two important things. The first is that Amazon Marketplace is a reverse auction in which sellers reduce prices until a sale is made. The second is that I was selecting exactly the wrong kind of books.

The fiction books that I've personally enjoyed reading are typically ones that lots of other people have liked too. As a result, thousands of copies were printed and sold, and hundreds of them have eventually appeared as used books in Amazon Marketplace.

As their popularity has faded, the prices of these used copies have fallen, sometimes to the penny level. Thus selecting books to sell based on my personal taste was not a viable business strategy.

Trying a Different Approach

Now that I understood about the reverse auction system, I relisted some of my previous inventory with closer attention to pricing and set aside the remaining books as valueless from a monetary standpoint, if not from a literary one! Steve's book recommends several categories of nonfiction books that I'd ignored, such as self-help, and also gives examples of esoteric books for which there's a market. After reading his chapter on inventory selection, I changed my searching to concentrate on older hardcover books, although I also purchased some paperbacks that seemed out-of-the-ordinary.

I also consulted Steve's appendix on descriptive terminology for books and tried to write more complete and professional descriptions. I expanded my inventory to 100 books. One of these was a paperback on Jungian psychology I found at a thrift store for a couple of bucks that sold for $5 only 5 hours after I listed it! I'd taken care to price my copy at the very bottom of the list. Certain the profit wasn't fabulous, but this almost instantaneous sale certainly showed me that there's a market out there!

This encouraged me to expand my inventory further and set up a book rack (I'd been using boxes before) to make it easier to find a specific book when an order came in. After a month and a half of encouraging sales, some at prices ranging from $80 to $120 for books I'd paid $2 or $3 for, I felt I'd gotten the basics of online bookselling figured out and started planning how I could expand my inventory to 1500 books.

Then, quite unaccountably from my standpoint, my sales slumped dishearteningly!

The Recurring Enigma of Slow Sales

My sales dropped almost to zero for an entire month, and I was baffled as to why, especially since I'd just expanded my inventory and thought I'd been doing a good job of selecting, describing, and pricing books based on my initial sales. I started to spend more time reading the Amazon seller discussion boards, which I hadn't felt the need to do before.

I wasn't encouraged to read in Steve Weber's blog that he was experiencing slow sales too, and that his Memorial Day weekend of 2007 was "the slowest in memory." Some other sellers were wondering about slow sales, too, although a few said theirs were normal.

A number of explanations were suggested for those reporting slow sales. Amazon.com had been having some technical problems ("unplanned events" in Amazon's terminology) around that time, and some sellers thought these glitches had impaired purchases. Some sellers mentioned a seasonal slump, but said that was usually in March and April, when my sales were strongest. Others suggested that there's a sales curve for any particular starting inventory, which gets "cherry picked" early on, and then sales drop off. Still others attributed slow sales and falling prices to a big increase in the number of sellers, especially "hobby sellers" who sell for fun, even if it's at a loss.

The only real solution that anyone proposed was adding fresh inventory, and I'd already tried that with little success. The one hopeful glimmer was that the few sales that I had were of books I'd come to think would never sell, for example, an imperfect 1924 hardcover copy of an obscure book called *The Constant Nymph*, which I'd been dismayed to find had been reissued in paperback in 2005! This book was one that I'd purchased on impulse for $1 at a garage sale. Despite its disclosed flaws, it eventually sold for $15 to a buyer in a neighboring state!

A nasty slump in sales after an encouraging start turns out to be a phenomenon frequently reported by sellers on the Amazon boards, and I'll explore the possible reasons for this in greater detail in a later chapter.

And I've subsequently experienced occasional and equally disheartening sales slumps. I'll discuss this topic further in a later chapter.

CHAPTER 10

Some Related Topics

In this section I discuss several topics related to online bookselling, including the increasing use of RFID tags by libraries and the increasing sales of ebooks, and then return to the demographic backdrop issue of the aging of the Baby Boomers.

What About RFID Tags?

A number of library systems are starting to place RFID (Radio Frequency IDentification) tags in books to automate checkout, return, and inventory management. These tags basically encode a unique identification number which can use to track a physical object such as a book or an item of merchandise. A special wireless scanner can be used to query tags and obtain their numbers, which can then be checked against a database.

In theory a book scout could take a handheld RFID scanner to a library book sale and use it to quickly and easily find books of particular interest or value. Because it's wireless rather than optical, individual books don't have to be held up to an RFID scanner – you can just point it at a shelf from a short distance away and get back a list of the books on that shelf.

The price of RFID tags and scanners has been falling (and their size has been shrinking), because they use semiconductor technology and benefit directly from the operation of Moore's Law. This has led to an increasing number of libraries switching to RFID tags, which means that more and more books now carry them.

From an online bookseller's standpoint, this technology is far from a clear win, however. The reason for this is that, unlike ISBNs, RFID codes are not standardized. There are at least half a dozen manufacturers of tags and scanners, and in general one manufacturer's scanner won't read another's tags.

Beyond this, knowing a book's RFID tag number doesn't help if you don't have access to the library's database containing information about it. Possibly some libraries will make their databases publicly available or sell access to them, but that of course would raise privacy concerns, since those databases might also contain records of who had checked out what book when, information that U.S. libraries have been very reluctant to release, even to the Office of Homeland Security. Some libraries might also erase the tracking numbers of books from their databases when they remove them from circulation and set them aside for a library sale to avoid future confusion.

Thus, useful as RFID tags are becoming for libraries, they are not automatically a boon for booksellers. Large bookstore chains like Borders and Barnes and Noble may also start to use RFID tags for inventory control, resulting eventually in large numbers of used books carrying them, but these chains may not be anxious to help used booksellers who compete with them by finding and reselling used books originating in their stock.

What About Ebooks?

One topic that's related to technological innovation and Moore's law is electronic books ("ebooks"). This is a topic about which I can write knowledgeably because I've been an ebook publisher for more than 10 years and have released more than 50 titles in several different reading device formats.

With the advent of the Amazon Kindle ebook reading device and more recently its follow-ons such as the Kindle 2 and the Kindle DX, ebooks indeed began to find market acceptance. Now, with the excitement generated by cool new reading devices like the Apple iPad and the Barnes and Noble Nook, ebooks are beginning to pose serious competition for new print books. However, that doesn't mean that they pose equally serious competition for the used print books offered by online booksellers.

One reason is the initial price of the Kindle and its competitors. Microminiaturization and the development of E-Ink technology have made possible the development of light handheld devices with long battery life and a more "paper-like" display that uses reflected rather than transmitted light. However, innovative technology usually isn't cheap, and a common complaint about ebook reading devices is their price.

And some people simply dislike reading on a screen. A key illustration of this is the 2004 book *The 9/11 Commission Report*, which sold hundreds of thousands of copies in print form even though it was available to read for free online. In this context, it's interesting to note that Michael Mould's *Online Bookselling* was first released as an ebook on CD-ROM and Mould only released a print edition because customers requested one.

Another reason that ebooks aren't likely to pose a big threat to online sales of used books anytime in the near future is that few publishers' full backlists are available as ebooks. For example, at the time of this writing the Kindle Store lists not a single one of J. K. Rowling's immensely popular Harry Potter books. That means that ebook reading devices will have zero impact on the sales of used copies of the Harry Potter series.

And simple automated scanning of a book's pages isn't sufficient to create a professional-quality ebook edition. Buyers of an ebook edition of, say, Grisham's *The Pelican Brief* will expect it be free of the typographical errors so often introduced by optical character recognition.

Buyers will also expect an ebook edition of a backlist book to have the same quality professional layout as a current bestseller released after the publisher had integrated ebook editions into an electronic publishing process. In many cases, a publisher will decide that the expense of issuing a quality ebook edition of an out-of-print book is prohibitive in view of projected sales.

Beyond this, books with large color pictures don't lend themselves to ebook editions. These books include art and architecture books, gardening books, travel books, and some cookbooks. Although the Apple iPad with its attractive screen display may change this, to the extent that ebooks have been successful historically, it's been primarily in the science fiction and romance genres, which leaves lots of genres to print books.

Amazon.com lists over 10 million books, and the Kindle store has only 300,000 ebooks. That's a tremendous number of books that are only available in print editions, and with many of these it will be decades before anyone takes the trouble to create an ebook edition of them.

Beyond that, collectible books are like antiques – a modern reproduction just isn't the same. The types of books that sellers report bringing especially good prices will, for the most part, continue to do so. Low-priced used copies of popular books will also continue find a market because they're cheaper than the corresponding ebook editions.

And some people won't buy ebooks because you can't usually loan them to someone else when you've finished them, as you can physical books. Others will prefer print books because of the reliability of future access – I can be assured that a print book that I set on my shelf 20 years ago and now want to refer to or reread will still be accessible to me. In contrast, consider a word processing document that I saved on whatever computer I may have been using 20 years ago and now want to look at. I may well find I can no longer open it for any of a variety of esoteric technical reasons. The same could be true for an ebook purchased today if I want to reread it 20 years from now.

The Aging of the Baby Boomers

The U.S. baby boomer generation is beginning to enter retirement age. In my geographic area, and probably in most other major urban areas as well, some of the most visible evidence of this profound demographic change is the construction of numerous big new retirement apartment complexes, often with provision for assisted living as well, in preparation for a big surge in demand for this type of accommodation. It also seems to me that I'm seeing more yard sales starting on

Fridays, reflecting more retired sellers and shoppers with leisure time during the week as well as on the weekend.

A significant segment of the baby boomer generation is relatively affluent and technology-savvy. Baby boomers are proving to be more health-conscious than their parents and they've also benefitted from advances in medical science, so their life expectancy is good.

My crystal ball is quite murky here, so I'll simply set out several different scenarios for how this demographic shift might affect the online bookselling business. The key point I want to make here is simply that there will assuredly be changes as a result of this impending demographic phenomenon.

Scenario 1 - Upsurge in Demand for Books

In this scenario, as baby boomers retire and find they have plenty of leisure time, they set out to catch up on their reading. Technology-savvy, well-equipped with powerful computers and broadband Internet connections, and used to shopping online, they turn to the Web to find the books they want to read. The result is a big upsurge in demand for books from online sellers. Strong demand drives up prices and online booksellers benefit.

Scenario 2 – Increased Supply of Used Books

In this scenario, as retiring baby boomers move from houses into apartments and condos, they don't have room for all the possessions they've gradually accumulated, books among them. They divest themselves of their less-treasured books by selling them at yard sales, giving them to their children or their friends, and donating them to Friends of Libraries groups and thrift stores. This increase in the supply of used books drives down prices and online booksellers suffer.

Scenario 3 – Lots More Online Booksellers

Looking for enjoyable hobbies and ways to bring in a little supplementary income, numerous retiring baby boomers take up online bookselling, attracted by the low barriers to entry and glowing accounts of financial success. The result is a surge in the number of online booksellers, increasing the competition for existing sellers.

Scenario 4 – A Composite of the First Three Scenarios

What's most likely, of course, is that each of these scenarios will play out to one degree or another, subjecting the online book business to an interplay of forces increasing demand, increasing supply, and intensifying competition simultaneously. That's what makes the overall outcome difficult to project from my personal vantage point.

CHAPTER 11

A Young Business

Reading the voluminous, constantly active Amazon sellers discussion boards with their frequent complaints about recent detrimental changes, it would be easy to forget that the online bookselling business is quite new on the scene. Little more than a decade ago, as discussed by Chris Anderson in *The Long Tail: Why the Future of Business Is Selling Less of More,* used books were sold primarily through bricks-and-mortar bookstores.

A Tale of Two Booksellers

When I think of the emergence of the online bookselling business, I think of two booksellers I know. The first is a fellow I've known for years who 20 years ago opened a bricks-and-mortar used bookstore in a small urban business district with high foot traffic. He was extremely knowledgeable about the business, had already acquired a good inventory, and certainly had customers, but rent increases soon made survival at his location an economic struggle. After a few years he moved to a lower-rent location nearby.

I lost touch with him for about 15 years and when I talked with him 8 years ago he was discouraged and just closing his bricks-and-mortar store. However, I now run into him from time to time at estate and library sales – he's switched entirely to online bookselling, which frees him to seek out valuable books for his inventory, and my impression is that he's doing well. "Amazon gets a lot of traffic," he tells me.

The second is a bookseller with a cozy bricks-and-mortar store in another small urban business district, one with low foot traffic compensated for by good parking. This district has several used bookstores within a few blocks, so it's something of a magnet for folks in the market for used books. This bookseller is a retired sea captain, so his bookstore is presumably not his sole source of income.

When I first dropped in several years ago, I was impressed that he clearly was tuned into the online bookselling world. When I asked about a particular book he didn't have in stock, he quickly checked AbeBooks and told me he could get a copy for me and how much it would cost. I know that today he sells online in Amazon Marketplace and, I presume, through many other online distribution channels as well.

In his case, I suspect that his primary source of income is online sales and that walk-in sales are gravy, so a low-traffic location with its accompanying low rent is a viable business strategy for him. In between walk-in customers he can work on filling orders and managing his inventory. Thus he's apparently been successful in combining a traditional used bookstore with online bookselling.

A Weakness of Amazon Marketplace

My SCORE business counselor is an avid and wide-ranging reader. When I talked with him about online bookselling just after getting started with it, he'd just read Thomas Friedman's *The World Is Flat: A Brief History of the Twenty-First Century.* A retired, highly computer-literate aircraft engineer turned business executive, he'd found what Friedman had to say so important that he'd decided to buy a copy for each of his four sons.

He immediately turned to Amazon Marketplace, where he knew he could often find good prices on used books. Sure enough, he found a seller offering a good price and started to place his order. Then he discovered that seller only had one copy. He would have to order a copy from each of four different sellers and pay a separate shipping cost for each copy.

This wasn't what he was looking for, and points up a weakness in Amazon Marketplace – it's great for buying one copy of a book, but most sellers (myself included) will seldom want to keep more than one copy of any particular book in their inventory, and it's difficult to find those who do. (There is actually a way to find a seller offering multiple copies of a book described on the

Amazon seller boards, but it's so esoteric and limited as to be almost irrelevant to the average customer.)

Examples of Business Complexity

I've already discussed the complexity created by the "book universe." Here are a few examples of other aspects of business complexity, some of which will be discussed in greater detail later on.

Unique Features of Distribution Channels

In addition to Amazon Marketplace, there are at least half a dozen other important distribution channels for online bookselling, including AbeBooks, Alibris, Biblio, eBay, Half.com, and ValoreBooks. Sellers using them report that certain types of books sell faster and/or at higher prices in one than another. However, each has its own subscription and fee structure, so differences in the cost of sales must be taken into consideration in comparing channels.

Using Multiple Distribution Channels

One nice thing about online bookselling is that you don't have to limit yourself to a single distribution channel, and many booksellers utilize multiple channels. The obvious advantage of this strategy is that listings reach a broader market. A subtle complexity however, is that running multiple, independent listings for a single book opens the possibility of two orders being placed for it on different channels because a sale on one doesn't automatically update the database on the other.

Third Party Software and Services

To make life more complicated yet, beyond the distribution channels are third party products, including software and services, that may help with various aspects of business. One example here is products and services to simplify listing the same inventory in a number of different distribution channels. A further complexity in this category is that some distribution channels are reported by sellers to be substantially slower than others in updating their databases, which can be an issue when a single copy of a book that sells rapidly is listed in multiple channels.

Dimensions of Complexity

As can be seen from the examples, there are a number of different sources of complexity in online bookselling. Here are a few of the more important dimensions of this complexity.

CHAPTER 12

Back to Amazon Marketplace

Now that I've covered some broader topics related to Amazon bookselling, it's time to return to the subject of Amazon Marketplace.

Online Bookseller Culture

I've already touched on certain aspects of online bookseller culture in previous chapters. Here I'll elaborate a little more.

A Quiet Trade

There are said to be about 40,000 booksellers on Amazon Marketplace at the moment. Every major city probably has several hundred, perhaps even several thousand in major metropolitan areas like New York and Los Angeles. However, unlike lawyers or real estate agents, most of these online booksellers don't advertise their presence except through their book listings, and you'd hardly know they're there. You won't see full-page newspaper ads or hear radio commercials telling you that you can make a fortune risk-free by buying and selling used books!

The exception to this rule of general anonymity is, of course, owners of bricks-and-mortar used bookstores, who generally also sell online these days and certainly advertise the presence of their stores. However, even these bookstore owners usually keep a low personal profile when they're out shopping for stock. You can get an idea how many there are in your area by going to a big library fundraising book sale, if there is one, and seeing how many people are industriously buying boxes and boxes of books, or by looking in the phone book under used bookstores.

At a thrift store, the person you see loading books into a shopping cart is almost certainly a dealer, perhaps strictly online or perhaps with a physical store. If you go to an estate sale, the person who's first in the door, goes straight to the books, and leaves 10 minutes later with an armload of them is unquestionably a dealer.

Why So Quiet?

There's a reason for keeping this low profile when buying books. In some lines of endeavor, like selling Amway, every person you meet is a potential customer. However, in online bookselling, every person you meet is far more likely to be a potential competitor than a customer because tastes in books are highly individual and the barriers to entry into the business are quite low. Beyond that, someone you run into at an estate sale isn't too likely to offer you the $15 you hope to get for a book online when they've just seen you buy it, along with a dozen others, for $1 apiece.

For this reason most of these dealers and online booksellers dress casually, are quiet and unobtrusive, and work solo. If you ask one of these people about bookselling as a business, they'll probably be too busy sifting through books to reply, and if they say anything at all, it will probably be brief and vague.

CHAPTER 13

Online Distribution Channels

Amazon Marketplace is at this point acknowledged as the preeminent distribution channel for online booksellers. As even a quick glance at the Amazon Seller Forums will confirm, it's a system with plenty of intricacies.

However, there are also a number of competing distribution channels, some well-established and some new on the scene, including AbeBooks, Alibris, Biblio, eBay, Half.com, and ValoreBooks. Life would be simpler if each were simply a clone of Amazon Marketplace and operated in exactly the same way.

Instead, however, each has its own subscription and fee structure, etc. Here are some details about some of these channels.

Half.com

One supplementary online distribution channel frequently mentioned in connection with Amazon Marketplace in seller discussions is Half.com, which has some definite strengths but a checkered history.

The Business Trajectory of Half.com

Between 1999 and 2003, Half.com was the favored distribution channel for used books, and many online sellers relied on it exclusively. In 2003 Half.com was acquired by eBay. Contrary to seller expectations, it faded rather than blossomed, and over the next year or so was largely superseded by Amazon Marketplace, to the point that it was slated for closure in 2005.

However, its scheduled demise was averted at the last moment and it continued to operate, but as a pale shadow of its former self from a bookseller standpoint. As late as February, 2007, sellers were uniformly lamenting their poor sales there in online discussions. However, by May, 2007, reports had become much more optimistic and at this point Half.com appears to be experiencing a resurgence. If you're thinking about selling on Half.com, check the Amazon seller discussion boards to find out if that resurgence has been successfully sustained or not.

Advantages of Half.com

It appears that today very few sellers rely exclusively on Half.com as their sole distribution channel, and many of its original sellers have abandoned it completely with the emergence of Amazon Marketplace. To most sellers, its appeal at this point seems to be as a supplementary channel rather than as their primary one.

One appealing aspect of Half.com is economic – like basic selling on Amazon Marketplace, it has no monthly subscription fee and no listing fees. It does charge a final value fee of 15% on each sale.

Another appealing aspect is convenience – listings don't expire, and if you already sell on eBay, your username and feedback rating appear automatically. You do have to register separately to start listing books on Half.com even if you already have an eBay account, however.

It's relatively easy to get started because many aspects of the Half.com system are similar to Amazon Marketplace, which is said to have used Half.com as a model. One downside is that the listing process, although quite similar, is slightly different from that used by Amazon Marketplace, and a duplicate set of listings has to be set up and maintained. For example, if you change a book's price in Amazon Marketplace, you need to remember do it in Half.com too.

Half.com does provide a tool called File Exchange to upload a batch of listings if they're first set up in a database or spreadsheet format and exported to a particular data interchange format (CSV, or comma separated value format, is one option; tab-separated format is another). However, if you're not already an established, fairly high-volume seller on eBay, you'll need to request special permission from customer support to get access to it.

One Major Drawback of Half.com

One major drawback of Half.com to be aware of is that it has a long list of things that can't be sold on the site, and one of them is "out-of-print books without ISBNs." This basically means any book published prior to about 1970, and hence rules out most collectible and all antiquarian books. For example, I have an interesting 1935 hardcover edition of Jules Verne's *The Mysterious Island*, but I can't list it on Half.com because the only editions available are recent paperback ones.

Other Sales Distribution Channels

I'll list some other major sales distribution channels, but I won't say much about them because I don't yet have any personal experience in using them. Consult the Amazon seller discussion boards and other books for current information about them, since changes in commisions and fees may have occurred since the time of this writing.

Alibris

Alibris is oriented toward antiquarian and collectible books. In 2011 it formed a partnership with Borders Books with the intent of challenging Amazon Marketplace. It charges a 15% commission with a $60 cap plus $1 a sale transaction fee for sellers subscribing to its $19.95 basic annual membership program. This program includes automatic listing of books on a number of partner websites, including Barnes & Noble, Borders, and Half.com. However, the commission for books sold on those sites is 20% rather than 15%.

For sellers having an Amazon Pro Merchant account, Amazon is also a partner website. Unlike Amazon orders, which are always shipped directly to the customer who purchases them, Alibris orders are sometimes for shipment to an Alibris distribution center. And unlike Amazon, Alibris may prohibit books with remainder marks.

In June, 2008, a new seller reported that "Alibris sales seem to be A LOT lower than Amazon" and another seller responded "Alibris sales are generally much less than Amazon's for us and I believe most sellers." If so, why bother to pay a subscription fee and list books there? In February, 2008, an Amazon forum contributor said, "I . . . get about 1 sale there for every 3-6 sales on Amazon, but the higher priced ones sell better there."

Biblio

Biblio has a very nice website and some very attractive aspects. Its biggest drawback at the time of this writing is that early on online booksellers reported that a very low percentage of their sales were through Biblio. However, that may be changing. And it's worth noting that in February, 2006, one Amazon forum contributor reported that "two of my highest priced sales this year have been on Biblio."

Biblio doesn't charge for listings, has a 15% commission with a cap of $40 for a basic seller account, allow sellers to set their own shipping fee, and doesn't charge a commission on shipping. It also has a rewards program that lowers fees for sellers with high customer satisfaction ratings. Biblio also makes available free software called BookHound for managing listings. BookHound has both Mac and PC versions.

AbeBooks

In 2008 AbeBooks was acquired by Amazon.com, which announced at that time that it planned to maintain AbeBooks as a separate and independently-operated entity.

In February, 2006, an Amazon forum contributor said, "The general consensus is that ABE is great for collectible fiction (expensive first editions, etc) but not so good for textbooks/technical books/bestsellers." Unlike Amazon, AbeBooks has monthly listing fees based on the number of books listed. The lowest level is $25 a month for up to 500 books. AbeBooks's commission is only 8%, but that's on the total amount of the order including shipping and expediting charges, not just on the price of the book, capped at $40. And there's also a 5.5% payment service fee on the total amount if payment is by credit card to AbeBooks. This is probably often the case, so the total commission is probably frequently 13.5%.

AbeBooks does provide free PC data management software called HomeBase and also supports FillZ, Web-based commercial listing management software that also works with Amazon, eBay, Alibris, Biblio, and a number of other distribution channels.

Increasingly Interwoven Distribution Channels

As is clear from the foregoing, there's a trend toward distribution channels becoming increasingly interwoven. While it's certainly possible to maintain separate accounts on multiple distribution channels and list inventory on each one, it's also possible to maintain a central inventory and sell on multiple distribution channels.

One advantage of this is that when a book listed on multiple distribution channels sells on one of them, it can be automatically removed from sale on each of the others. Updating all the distribution channels isn't instantaneous, though, so it's definitely possible to receive a second order for a book that's already been sold.

Art of Books

Art of Books (familiarly known as AOB) is an inventory listing management service that links to Amazon, Alibris, AbeBooks, Half.com, and Biblio in addition to a number of other distribution changes. It charges only a 1% commission, but there's also a minimum of $10 per month. AOB provides proprietary inventory management and repricing software for PC and Mac.

Automatic Repricing of Books

A big topic in online bookselling is automatic repricing of books. I won't discuss the advantages and pitfalls of this here because I do strictly manual repricing and so have no experience with automatic repricing.

How Do Other Distribution Channels Compare to Amazon.com?

A logical question for the online bookseller is how different distribution channels compare in terms of sales. There's not a lot of information on this, and, of course, the type of inventory will figure in as well, but most online sellers agree that Amazon Marketplace is the most important distribution channel.

One Amazon Marketplace seller recently reported the following mid-2007 sales figures for an inventory that CDs, DVDs, VHS tapes, and audiobooks as well as books:

Distribution Channel	% of Sales
Amazon Marketplace	54.9
Half.com	34.3
AbeBooks	8.8
Alibris	2.0

Another Amazon Marketplace seller who didn't indicate their type of inventory other than to say that it included slow-selling books also reported mid-2007 sale figures. This set of figures is complicated by the fact that not all of their inventory is listed on the three sites they use.

Distribution Channel	% of Sales	Amount of Inventory Listed
Amazon Marketplace	44%	1/3
Half.com	29%	most
Alibris	26%	more than 1/3

Here's a report on mid-2007 sales from a third seller who didn't specify their type of inventory:

Distribution Channel	% of Sales
Amazon Marketplace	40.6
Half.com	26.9
eBay	12.2
Alibris	8.5
Barnes and Noble.com	7.9
Biblio	1.5
AbeBooks	2.2
ValoreBooks	0.3

Sales Pace and the Sales Curve

> "One of the biggest mistakes new online booksellers make is to assume that since they listed 200 books last week and have sold 50 of them, the other 150 will sell in another three weeks." – Mould (2006), p. 23

> "A newly acquired inventory has a sales curve . . . Everyone has the "honeymoon' period when the hot part of their inventory sells off . . ." – Amazon seller forum contributor, 2007

What is "the sales curve" and how does it relate to the pace of online book sales? The contributor quoted above gave the following example of what he or she means by "the sales curve," presumably based on his or her own recent experience, for the sales curve starting with an inventory of 1000 books.

Time	No. of Books Sold
First month	350
Second month	87
Third month	40
Fourth month	21

While other online booksellers might dispute the exact numbers, most would probably agree that older inventory sells more slowly because it's already been "cherry-picked" and that the concept of the sales curve is a valid one. What this means is that for a given inventory the pace of sales will gradually fall off. The conclusion usually drawn from this is that to sustain a certain level of sales it's important to keep adding to inventory.

CHAPTER 14

Sales Slumps

"No sales, she wails!" – Amazon seller forum contributor, 2007

Closely related to the topics of sales pace and the sales curve discussed in the previous chapter is the "sales holiday" or slump that many new online sellers, myself included, report experiencing a month or two after they start selling. I've described my own first experience with a sales slump in an earlier chapter. As it turns out, sales slumps are so common and so alarming that they're a frequent topic of discussion in the Amazon sellers forums.

To summarize my own early experience, after a first unproductive attempt to sell some books online on Amazon.com, I made a fresh start in early 2007, this time paying closer attention to competitive pricing, sales ranks, and descriptions. I expanded my inventory and found that my efforts were soon rewarded with much-improved sales. Encouraged by this initial success, I expanded my inventory still further and started organizing my storage system better. After a month and a half of continued modest success, I felt I'd mastered the basics of online bookselling and made plans to expand my inventory considerably.

Then, quite unaccountably from my standpoint, my sales slumped dramatically! Orders fell almost to zero for an entire month, and I was baffled as to why, since I now had a larger inventory to offer and thought I'd been doing a good job of selecting, describing, and pricing my books. To figure out what was going on, I started to spend more time reading the Amazon seller discussion boards, which I hadn't felt the need to do before. I was discouraged to read in Steve Weber's blog that he was experiencing slow sales just then too, and that his Memorial Day weekend of 2007 was "the slowest in memory." Some other sellers were wondering about slow sales, too, although a few said theirs were normal.

A number of explanations for such slow sales were suggested by forum contributors. Amazon.com had been having some technical problems ("unplanned events" in Amazon's terminology) around that time, and some sellers thought these glitches had disrupted purchases. Other sellers mentioned typically experiencing a seasonal slump, but said that was usually in March and April, when my own sales had been strongest. Still others blamed the sales curve associated with any particular starting inventory. The theory here is that an initial inventory gets "cherry-picked" early on and then sales drop off. However, the declining sales curve doesn't account for a sudden and prolonged drop in sales to zero! Yet other sellers attributed slow sales and falling prices to a big increase in the number of sellers, especially "hobby sellers" who sell for fun, even if it's at a loss. More sellers listing their inventories online means a greater supply of used books, resulting in lower sales and falling prices for established sellers if demand stays constant.

The proposed solution that found the most agreement in the forums at the time was to add fresh inventory to get around the declining sales curve problem. Another suggestion was reducing prices to keep them competitive, although that's something most sellers do routinely anyway. However, one seller said that repricing books either higher or lower helped her sales, she thought because a price change of any sort refreshes the listing. Another forum contributor suggested canceling book listings and then relisting them, again with the idea of refreshing each listing so that it appears before prior listings from other sellers at the same price point.

I tried all of these suggestions but found that none worked so miraculously for me that I could testify confidently to its success. My sales did eventually pick up again, but ever since I've periodically experienced occasional and equally disheartening sales slumps, even as

I've continued to add inventory steadily. One thing I start to wonder about when I go for weeks without a single sale is if somehow my Amazon inventory has vanished from the online listings! Then all of a sudden I'll get a sale, often followed by a flurry of additional sales over a period of several days, so I'm reassured that potential buyers are indeed seeing my listings. I've gradually gotten used to these slumps and attribute them to having an inventory that I'm intentionally shifting in the direction of esoteric books with a limited market.

However, an online bookseller friend with a large, varied inventory did tell me a couple of years ago that he'd just discovered that a large percentage of his listings had somehow vanished from Amazon's database, presumably due to some technical glitch. If you're concerned that this might have happened to you as well, try picking a few books from your inventory at random and searching for them to see if the listings are indeed appearing. If any significant number of listings have "evaporated," as my friend's did, it won't take you long to establish that.

CHAPTER 15

Pricing of Used Books

How do online booksellers price their books? This is another frequent topic of discussion in the Amazon sellers forums. Here I'll briefly discuss lowballing, penny book, what I'll term "highballing," the middle-price strategy I usually use myself, and repricing, both manual and automated.

Lowballing

Lowballing is the practice of pricing a book much lower than the cheapest comparable copy on the market, and it's a frequent cause of complaint by established sellers, who are horrified to another seller list a copy of a book for much less than the price they think it should command. In many cases this is presumably done by impatient sellers in the hopes of getting a quick sale, although it's unclear to me that desirable but slow-selling books are extremely price-sensitive. However, it can occur in other ways as well. In a few cases a strikingly low price is simply due to a typographical error. In other cases it's apparent that two sellers are competing aggressively by repeatedly underpricing each other, causing the price to fall precipitously.

How does lowballing happen? In many cases, lowballing is probably the result of automatic repricing software operating with no lower limit set. However, one seller reported that he unintentionally lowballed the price of a book by a factor of ten due to a typo in the decimal point of the price. The book sold before he caught the error, but rather than try to cancel the sale he simply chalked the mistake up to experience and filled the order.

Penny Books

An extreme case of lowballing is penny books, the nightmare of most sellers but the metier of a few, who have chosen seller names like "booksapenny." Most sellers consider that with Amazon fees they can't make a profit on a book selling for less than a certain amount, but a few have tried to figure out how to operate so efficiently that they can make a profit on the shipping allowance. Actually, penny books don't necessarily fall into the category of lowballing. In many cases the price simply reflects a very high supply relative to the demand.

If penny books are typically sold at a loss, what's the minimum price a seller needs to set in order to make a profit on a sale of a single book? That depends on several factors, starting with the acquisition cost of the book. The amount of the Amazon commission is obviously important and depends somewhat on the type of Amazon account you have. Shipping materials, if you're using purchased rather than recycled ones, is also an expense. Finally, there's the postage, which varies depending on the weight of the book, the method of shipment, and current postal rates. If you're fortunate enough to have gotten the book for quite cheaply, say $0.25 at a yard sale, it's of ordinary size and weight, and shipping is by Media Mail, the price at which you break even on the sale is likely to be between $3 and $4.

Highballing

What I'll term "highballing" isn't actually a general seller strategy, it's rather the observation that with many books there'll be one listed at what seems an unreasonably high price, say $250, when other copies are less than half that amount. It's hard to explain these prices or to know whether anyone ever buys one of these copies in preference to a much cheaper comparable one. Steven Windwalker has commented on these and all he can suggest is that they may have to do with money laundering. Rex Stout, Dorothy Sayers, and P. D. James all have mysteries based on illicit mail-order schemes involving over-priced merchandise shipped to a puzzling clientele.

Middle Price Strategy

As a general rule I price my own books within the range established by sellers who aren't clearly lowballers or highballers. I reason that if I underprice the lowest-priced seller, he or she will just reprice their book to underprice my listing. My hope is that for one reason or another a prospective purchaser scanning the listing will pick mine. Weber (2006) and Mould (2006) both recommend a middle-of-the-road pricing strategy.

Repricing Interval

If an online seller isn't using automatic repricing software, how often should they reprice their books? To me that's a difficult question to answer definitively because in my experience some books are price-sensitive and others are not. While one would think that buyers would generally purchase the lowest-priced copy listed, in practice some buyers evidently use other criteria than price and condition in selecting which copy to buy. For example, they might prefer to pay more for a copy from an established seller with good feedback than take the risk of saving money by buying from one who has disappointed some customers. In terms of my own inventory I haven't usually seen any immediate increase in sales when I've reduced prices. This is a topic where I'd definitely suggest reading comments and advice in the Amazon forums.

How often should an online bookseller reprice his or her offerings? Book prices definitely change with time, especially for current bestsellers. When a book first becomes a bestseller, a good used copy will often command a price close to half that of a new one. With the passage of time buyer interest will shift to newly-emerging bestsellers and used copies will flood into the marketplace, causing the price to drop rapidly, to the point where it may eventually become a penny book.

Mould (p. 69) recommends repricing books every 6 months. For some books I've done it as often as once every 2 months. However, many online sellers subscribe to automated repricing software and some set it to reprice their entire inventory as often as once a day.

Buying Low and Selling High

One question that arises from time to time in discussions of "lowballing" in the Amazon seller forums is why not buy ridiculously low-priced copies of books and resell them at a profit? A few sellers report actually doing this once in awhile, but others say that they consider it too risky because book prices can plummet rapidly if their popularity fades or more copies come flooding into the market.

CHAPTER 16

Expanding an Existing Online Bookselling Business

Suppose you've tested the waters of Amazon Marketplace for selling used books online by setting up a seller's account, listing some books (maybe ones you've bought, maybe just books you own already and are willing to part with), and establishing that you get enough sales to make the endeavor worth pursuing. What are your options for expanding your business further?

If you're getting sales, you've established that you're able to select books to list, to describe them adequately, and to price them competitively. You've probably also been getting good customer feedback and not having a lot of issues with customer returns or Amazon A-Z Claims, otherwise you'd be hearing from Amazon. If you're selling books you've bought for resale, not just books from your own personal collection, you've also identified sources of inventory, perhaps including thrift stores, Friends of Library sales, or estate sales, which you may or may not be satisfied with.

For purposes of this discussion, let's assume you've been operating on a shoestring and haven't invested in a barcode scanner or a subscription to an online cell phone scouting service, subscribed to an Amazon Pro

Merchant account, or subscribed to a service like Art of Books or AMan. At this point you're in a position to consider several alternative strategies, the most obvious being to increase sales volume.

A Straightforward Strategy: Increasing Sales Volume

The first strategy that's apt to come to mind for expanding an online bookselling business is to increase sales volume. There are two main options for increasing volume. The first is to increase inventory, reasoning that sales will go up in direct proportion to online offerings. The second is to market to more customers by expanding into additional distribution channels. In either case, you need to consider the issue of scaling.

The Problem of Scaling Up

One key issue to take into account in planning for increased sales volume is that of scaling up. Since it's the number of sales we're talking about increasing, perhaps dramatically, we need to keep in mind the time required to pick, pack, and ship each individual order and Amazon's two-business-day order fulfillment requirement. Increasing sales volume could cut into inventory acquisition, and a massive increase in sales volume could mean difficulty in fulfilling orders within two business days and possibly negative customer feedback.

Increasing Sales Volume and Increasing Operating Costs

Increasing sales volume can also increase operating costs in two different ways. Depending on your home's available storage space, increased inventory may require renting additional storage space. Expanding your market by adding distribution channels can increase operating costs by adding monthly subscription fees and possibly additional sales-related fees as well.

Additional Distribution Channels and Increasing Business Complexity

By their very nature each distribution channel is different in some significant way from all the others, which inevitably adds business complexity as channels are added. For example, some distribution channels may have quite different shipping requirements than others.

Inventory management also becomes more complex if specific books are listed in multiple channels, since a sale in one will not automatically update database information in others. There are several subscription services for online sellers that integrate inventory management for all the major distribution channels, but the increase in operating costs involved must be taken into consideration, especially since most sellers report that their sales through other channels are much smaller than those through Amazon Marketplace.

More Oblique Strategies

Less straightforward strategies to expanding an online business include investing in technology to increase productivity in various aspects of it. These aspects include inventory selection, which may include travel time and expense to sources of inventory; describing, pricing and listing; inventory management, including culling and periodic repricing; order fulfillment, which can be divided into picking, packing, and shipping; and post-sale customer service, including responding to emails from buyers about issues with orders.

One important example here is to increase productivity in inventory selection by investing in a handheld barcode scanner and subscribing to an online pricing service, with an attendant increase in operating costs. Another is increasing inventory quality and focusing on increasing the average price per sale as opposed to concentrating on increasing sales volume.

Developing a Business Plan

Do you need to develop a business plan for an online bookselling business? Probably not if it's just a hobby activity. A stamp collector who buys stamps for his or her personal collection, trades them with other collectors, and sells duplicates doesn't really need a business plan.

Where a business plan usually comes in is if you need financing like a bank loan to start up or expand a business activity. However, if you're thinking of expanding an existing online bookselling business (if you're reading this book, you've probably already started one), you may well want to develop a business plan for your own benefit even if you don't plan on seeking outside financing.

Mould's 2006 book goes into bookselling business plans for various target income levels in detail, and I won't spend a great deal of time on this topic here. However, I will suggest starting by doing what might be termed an "opportunity analysis," although some might consider it better termed strategic planning.

The point of this opportunity analysis to take some time to think about and write down what you have in mind, and parts of what you write can later be included in the narrative section of your business plan if you end up developing one to use in seeking outside financing. The process I'm suggesting here is somewhat akin to brainstorming in that you don't need to do online research or assemble a stack of reference books to do it – you just draw on what you've learned already. For this reason the process need not be time-consuming – half an hour to an hour may suffice – and you're only aiming for a rough draft, so you can come back and add or modify things later.

First, write a brief title that identifies the opportunity you see. This is really just a placeholder at this point, so it can be quite simple and vague, something along the lines of "Opportunity – Expand Existing Online Bookselling Business."

Begin by taking 5 to 10 minutes to write a brief background section. It's not necessary to be thorough or exhaustive here – the purpose is just to focus your thinking on the topic at hand. Here you would just put down a little about the history of your business, how it's developed, and how you see the industry of which it's a part.

Next, write a brief vision statement stating how you would ideally imagine your idea for taking advantage of the opportunity you've identified working out. Do your best to make it one sentence – a long, complex sentence is okay. This is what you would say to an audience if you were beginning a presentation of your idea.

Next, add two sections, one entitled "Pros" and the other "Cons." Start by listing things that come to mind in one category or the other – selling points for your idea and objections that others might raise to it. Often writing down a "pro" will immediately bring to mind a "con" or vice versa, so expect to bounce back and forth between the two lists adding things as they come to mind.

Finally, write down a list of things you would need to move forward on taking advantage of the opportunity or the next steps you would take to act on it. The goal of this process is to clarify your idea in your mind and ensure that you've considered it from several different angles.

The benefits are two-fold. First, working through this exercise will help keep you from being swept away by enthusiasm for your idea. Second, it will help keep you from being overly discouraged as objections to it occur to you. Notice that there is no final "go/no go "decision-making step – you can come back and add things to the analysis as often as you wish.

Here's a skeleton example to give you the general idea of how this works.

Opportunity – Expand Existing Online Bookselling Business

Background

I started online bookselling part-time six months ago and am encouraged by my success. At this point I feel that I've learned the business well enough that I can think about how to bring in more income.

Vision

Expand my online bookselling business to double my income

Pros

I feel confident that I'm well up the learning curve.

I've established a good track record as an online bookseller, so I think customers will be confident in buying from me.

I can read more about the business in books and on the Amazon seller discussion boards.

I can rent inventory storage space inexpensively if necessary.

Etc.

Cons

I'm concerned that there may still be pitfalls to the business that I haven't discovered yet.

I have limited space to store additional inventory and limited time buy books and fill orders.

Etc.

Next Steps

I can use my historical sales and costs information to set up balance sheets factoring costs of additional rental space for inventory storage and see what levels of income would be produced by different sales scenarios.

I should read current discussions on Amazon seller boards to see what issues other sellers are presently encountering.

CHAPTER 17

Some Minor Matters

Your Seller Name – How Much Does It Matter?

To register to sell on Amazon.com, you need to give a seller name, which can be the same as your customer name if you already have an Amazon account. If you're drafting a business plan, you'll probably want to give some thought to your seller name.

How much difference does a seller name make? Relatively little from my personal standpoint as a customer.

I find I pay much more attention to a book's price and condition and to the seller's feedback rating than I do to their online name. A "geeky" name doesn't bother me at all, and I don't attach too much significance to a name that implies an experienced, professional seller. However, I might be put off by a deliberately offensive seller name like "InYoFaceBooks".

Selecting Books to Buy

One recurring question on the Amazon discussion boards is where to find inventory. Mould gives a detailed list in his book, including local library fundraising shelves, community book sales, church fundraisers, thrift stores, bookstore clearance shelves and bargain tables, estate sales, and garage sales. The full list is too long to repeat here; see his chapter entitled "Where to Buy Your Inventory".

A related question is how to select books once you've arrived at, say, the book section of a thrift store. Mould says that he, like most beginners, started out with "blind buying," which he still resorts to at crowded library fundraising sales.

"Blind buying" is Mould's term for selecting books to purchase without checking their current price in online distribution channels. Selection criteria may be personal taste, sheer intuition, or previous experience in selling certain types of books.

The alternative is informed buying, in which the current values of individual books are checked prior to purchase. Mould emphasizes (p. 50) that to succeed at online bookselling, "You need to know the value of a book BEFORE you buy it."

There are various ways to do this. One common way is to subscribe to a cell phone service that enables you to look up current price information and sales rank for individual books based on their ISBN.

Diamonds in the Rough

Since I now specialize in collectible and antiquarian books, I've found other authors' lists of "diamonds in the rough" – unusually valuable and generally esoteric or obscure books – especially useful. Michael Mould has one such list entitled "Examples of Gems I Have Bought and Sold" on p. 73 of his book. This is a list of 15 books he purchased for prices ranging from $0.25 to $4.00 and sold for prices spanning the range $50 to $260.

Most are nonfiction and their subjects include real estate accounting, wind energy, and mechanical engineering (being himself a mechanical engineer in the aviation industry may give Mould an advantage in this last subject area).

Steve Weber has another list like this in his book. I won't repeat either of these lists here, and I've only found one of the specific books on them, but studying these lists has helped give me an idea of what kinds of books to keep an eye out for.

I've also compiled a list of books that brought prices of $100 or more on eBay which is available separately as an ebook to make it easy to carry along and refer to when out scouting for books. It's called *Some Ugly Ducklings Amongst Used Books, 2007*. Although it's far from current at this point, at least half the books listed are ones of enduring rather than ephemeral value.

Blink by Malcolm Gladwell

One interesting related topic is how a person can rapidly select books successfully *without* checking their value with a barcode scanner or cell-phone lookup service. Mould reports (p. 52) that one of his sons, a seasoned and highly successful online bookseller, attended a crowded university book sale where "based on his experience in determining book values, he loaded seven shopping carts with books," less than 2% of which turned out to be valueless ("firewood" is the term Mould likes to use), beating out other dealers using cell phones to look up prices. (Mould says that his own five years of experience aren't sufficient for him to duplicate this feat.)

How does an experienced dealer make snap decisions based on glancing at a book faster than a person can pick up a book, scan the barcode, and get a "beep" back through their headset? Malcolm Gladwell's book *Blink* is about "rapid cognition," the kind of thinking that happens in the blink of an eye.

Without going into detail here, I'll just say that one topic he discusses is what he calls "thin slicing," the ability of the unconscious to find patterns in situations and behavior based on very narrow slices of experience."

An example might be glimpsing the spine of a book and recognizing it as one of possible value.

Gladwell gives a number of examples of people's ability in certain situations to make accurate decisions by picking up on particular cues. There's no unerring magic here – he also gives examples of erroneous decisions made on the same basis.

Return Policy

How important is a seller's return policy? A couple of months after the incident just described I needed to buy a college mathematics textbook for my daughter, and a quick check showed much lower priced copies available in Amazon Marketplace than at our local university bookstore. In the past I've tended to order the lowest-priced copy of a book without paying much attention the seller's feedback, but this time as a result of my recent experience I was more cautious and gave the first few listings close scrutiny.

The lowest-priced copy was only in acceptable condition and I wanted a better one, so I moved on to another listing, which was only slightly more expensive. This seller had almost 600 lifetime feedback ratings and an average rating of 95% – not bad, but still low enough to want to take a close look at his or her feedback.

I looked over a few of the most recent pages of feedback and found that he or she posted their responses to negative feedback, which was definitely helpful in assessing its validity. In doing so, I found that most of the negative feedback concerned refusing to allow returns, perhaps a reasonable policy for a seller specializing in textbooks and worried that students will buy them, use them for a course, and then return them.

I was concerned, though, about being shipped the wrong book by mistake and having difficulty in returning it, so I looked at the feedback for another seller with a 95% average feedback rating, this one with over 1000 lifetime feedback ratings. This seller didn't post responses to negative feedback and a frequent complaint was that they also didn't respond to email. Another common complaint was that books arrived late or never arrived at all – not what I was looking for. I also passed over a seller with 900 lifetime ratings and a 92% average rating as well as one with over 15,000 lifetime ratings and a 96% average rating.

I finally settled on a new seller with only 3 lifetime feedback ratings but a 100% average rating. The feedback left for him mainly mentioned rapid delivery of the book. I reasoned that a new seller would be more likely to be responsive if an issue arose with the order and purchased his copy. My choice was reasonable in that the book did arrive on schedule and in good condition.

Moral of the story: A new seller can get my personal Amazon book order over even a long-established one – a long track record and lots of sales don't confer an automatic compelling advantage. On the other hand, I would have been reluctant to buy from a "just launched" seller.

If you're particularly interested in this topic, I suggest searching the Amazon sell forums for "returns".

CHAPTER 18

A Few Tips

In this section I give a few tips about online selling on Amazon, some based on my own experience and others picked up from the Amazon seller forums.

An Amazon Catch-22 to Avoid

Amazon polices its Marketplace sellers to at least some small degree, and, for various reasons, at least occasionally bars someone permanently from selling. It's hard to judge how often this actually occurs, perhaps only very rarely, but there are periodically anguished posts in the sellers' forums reporting that this has occurred.

Obviously an online bookseller wants to avoid even the remote possibility of being permanently barred from selling, which is usually the result of Amazon's judgment that a seller is a scam artist. However, for understandable reasons, Amazon doesn't disclose exactly how it determines that someone is a scammer.

It appears that one way is by checking for people using different identities to open seller accounts. This is determined by noticing that two seller accounts are being used from a single computer, for example if a husband and wife have separate seller accounts. For this reason, it's essential for members of the same household to be scrupulously careful to use separate computers if they have separate seller accounts.

Some people also report that they believe that they were barred from selling because they had accessed their seller account from public computer at a library or a Kinko's. If another Amazon Marketplace seller has previously used the same computer, that might be picked up by Amazon.

The safest thing to do if you need to access your Amazon seller account from several different locations is to take a laptop computer with wi-fi capability with you, since many public libraries and some coffee shops offer free wi-fi. In the Seattle area even some Safeway and Fred Meyer stores offer free wi-fi ("Make your shopping trip even more productive!").

For more information about this topic, search the Amazon new seller board for "banned", "account", "blocked", and "violations"

The Lessons Learned Log

Because of the complexities of the online bookselling business, it's difficult to avoid making at least an occasional mistake in some aspect of it. My personal practice is, when I make a new kind of mistake, whether in inventory selection, shipping, or whatever, to log it in a "Lessons Learned" file. I just write a brief entry about it that I can reread if I feel a need to jog my memory at some future time.

Packing Books

I don't know what my book packages look like when they arrive, but I do know how books I buy come through the mail. In my observation, Amazon Marketplace sellers use a wide variety of methods for packaging books, and in general there are a wide range of methods, including boxes, bubble-pack envelopes, and corrugated cardboard packaging, that all seem to work pretty well most of the time.

However, I have received a couple of books in partially torn envelopes. This seems to happen primarily when the envelope is much larger than the book so it can "rattle around" inside it in transit.

There are two big concerns with rattling around. The first is damage to what was possibly originally a nice book. The second is the book coming out of the envelope entirely and being lost. Either way, as a seller you're going to have to answer emails from the customer and possibly having to ship a replacement copy or issue a refund.

For my part, if I ship an expensive book, I certainly want it to arrive undamaged. Beyond that, I want the customer to feel that care was taken to pack the book well.

If I ship an inexpensive book, I prefer to use adequate but inexpensive packaging. However, the last thing I want is to have to spend a lot of time resolving an issue with a lost or damaged inexpensive book. Thus I want to be sure to avoid that torn envelope!

The seller of one book I received recently solved this problem neatly by cutting the bottom of the bubble pack envelope to form a second flap at the end and folding this flap over the end of the book. Then she folded the end of the envelope down to shorten it to fit the book and used the adhesive strip to seal it as usual. The end result was a short, sturdy envelope just the right length for the book.

The best packaging materials and methods are a subject of frequent debate on the Amazon discussion boards, and I won't go into the subject in detail here. If you're interested in finding out about extremely secure ways of packaging books, whether you choose to use them or not, I suggest reading the section on wrapping books in Michael Mould's book and searching for "book AND burrito" and for "packaging" in the Amazon sellers forums.

Shipping Books Internationally

I usually offer international shipping for the books I list on Amazon and have been very pleased to get sales from international purchasers, mainly in Canada and

Europe but occasionally in Australia or Japan. However, as other sellers have commented from time to time in the Amazon forums, for the most part it only makes sense to offer international shipping for books that will fit in a USPS Priority Mail Flat-Rate Envelope. That's because Amazon's shipping allowances aren't based on the weight or size of the book. The shipping allowance for an international sale is about the price of mailing a flat-rate envelope. It the book is too big to fit in one, then it must be shipped by Priority Mail at a cost about 3 times that of a flat-rate envelope or by another carrier such as UPS. If the book is a valuable one that's not a major issue, but if it's not it's quite possible that the sale will be at significant loss to the seller.

The Amazon Vacation Setting

One advantage of Amazon Marketplace is that you can put your sales on hold temporarily if you have a reason to do so. This is done by going "on vacation", although of course you might simply be ill or too busy with other activities to fill orders within the two business days Amazon requires.

If orders come in before the setting takes effect that you aren't able to fill within the normal two business days of being placed, you will probably have some annoying issues to deal with when you resume online bookselling. However, it's best to plan for going on vacation a couple of days in advance, since the setting can take up to 36 hours to activate. For more on this topic, search the Amazon seller forums for "vacation."

The "Frozen" Order

Occasionally if you login to your Amazon seller account you make notice a new order listed that you haven't received a notification email about and that hasn't shown up in ASON (Amazon Services Order Notifier). It can sit there for a day or two, seemingly inexplicably frozen in time, and you may wonder if there's a glitch in Amazon's automatic notification system.

In actuality this is a normal but infrequent occurrence when a buyer's credit card purchase takes a long time to clear. The order is logged but not processed until the funds are received by Amazon. As soon as that happens, you'll receive the normal notifications and can proceed to fill it. You can get more information about this by searching the Amazon seller forums for "clear."

ASON Issues

Amazon is not a major Windows software company, but it has released a downloadable piece of PC software called ASON (Amazon Services Order Notifier). The idea of ASON is to provide Marketplace sellers with a channel for order information that is more secure than email. However, from time to time sellers have reported various issues with ASON, including crashes, order notification delays, and incompatibility with Windows Vista. If you're a new Marketplace seller and have just installed ASON, I'd definitely suggest searching for "ASON" on the Amazon discussion boards to familiarize yourself with any technical issues with this software that users are presently reporting.

CHAPTER 19

33 Valuable Used Books

Each of these 33 easily overlooked used books has sold for $100 or more on eBay in the past few years. Note that these are books you might actually encounter at yard sales, etc., as opposed to rare and antiquarian books, which are primarily signed first editions.

Hardcover

Brian Lumley, *The Source*, 1998, TOR, 1st edition, $105

Terry Pratchett, *Once More with Footnotes*, 2004, Nesfa Press, 1st edition, 3rd printing, ISBN 1886778574, $213

Cormac McCarthy, *Child of God*, 1974, Random House, 1st edition, ISBN 0394487710, $532

Sax Rohmer, *Insidious Dr. Fu Manchu*, 1920's, A.L. Burt, $188

Clive Cussler, *The Mediterranean Caper & Iceberg*, 1995, Scribner, ISBN 0684825996, $119

Agatha Christie, *Black Coffee*, 1998, Bantam/Literary Express, 1st edition, $100

Victor Hugo, *The Man Who Laughs*, 1928, Grosset and Dunlap, $105

Marcel Proust, *Selected Letters, Vol. III*, 1992, Harper Collins, $110

June Hemmons Hiatt, *The Principles of Knitting*, 1988, Simon & Schuster, $167

Alice Starmore, *Fair Isle Knitting*, 1994, Taunton Press, ISBN 0918804973, $150

Mary Walker Phillips, *Creative Knitting, a New Art Form*, 1971, $199

Dale P. Clemens, *Custom Rod Thread Art*, 1982, RodCrafters Press, 1st edition, $125

John T. Spike, *Fairfield Porter: An American Classic*, 1992, Abrams, $187

Andrew Loomis, *Successful Drawing*, 1951, 1st edition, $175

John Canemaker , *Treasures of Disney Animation Art*, 1992, ISBN 0896600319, $105

Melissa Gabardi, *Art Deco Jewellery 1920-1949*, 1989, THE ANTIQUE COLLECTORS' CLUB, $159

Alexander Von Solodkoff, *The Jewel Album of Tsar Nicholas II*, 1997, 1st edition, $108

Richard Schmid, *Richard Schmid Paints Landscapes*, $129

Ronald W. Lightbown, *Art of Mantegna*, 1986, University of California Press, ISBN 0520056582, $205

Alla Rosenfeld, Norton T. Dodge, *Nonconformist Art*, 1995, Thames & Hudson, ISBN 0500237093, $125

Howard Harlan and W. Anderson, *Duck Calls: An Enduring American Folk Art*, 1988, 1st edition, $165

Jeff Ellis, *The Clubmaker's Art*, 1997, Zephyr Productions, ISBN 096530390X, $177

Frederic Katz, *Art Arfons Fastest Man on Wheels*, 1964, Rutledge Books, 1st edition, $139

Paperback

Richard Bachman, Stephen King, *Rage*, 1983, New English Library, ISBN 0450053792, $152

Stephen King, *Startling Mystery Volume One, #6, "The Glass Floor"*, 1967, $300

Craig Harrison, *The Quiet Earth*, 1986, $150

Kiera Dellacroix, *Engravings of Wraith*, $183

R.S.Corliss, *Conspiracy of Swords*, $108

George Robert Elford, *Devil's Guard*, 1981, NEL, $102

John L. Parker, Jr., *Once a Runner*, 1998, Cedarwinds, ISBN 0915297019, $229

Alice Starmore, *Tudor Roses*, 1998, Unicorn Books, ISBN 0962558680, $160

Syd Mead, *Sentinel*, 1979, 1st edition, $122

Donald Farr, *Mustang BOSS 302*, 1983, 1st edition, $212

CHAPTER 20

Conclusion

Perhaps the most important conclusion to be drawn here is the inevitability of change in the online bookselling business. Reading some of the comments by veteran online booksellers in the Amazon seller forums decrying changes of one sort or another, I sometimes wonder if they've forgotten that it was a huge change, the rise of the Internet, that made it possible for this business to exist in the first place! Online bookselling, whether as a profession, an avocation, or source of supplemental income, owes its existence to the advancement of computer and network technology, and that advancement continues today and will continue with the passage of time, likely even at an increased pace.

The change that would threaten the existence of the online bookselling business is the collapse of the market for used books, and even with the increasing popularity of ebooks that doesn't seem to be even a remote possibility. Ebooks will no doubt reduce the market for used copies of current bestsellers to some degree, but many fairly recent out-of-print books will never be made available as ebooks.

Demographic factors, particularly the aging of the Baby Boomers, will also change the online market for used books, but exactly how is something my crystal ball is far too murky to predict.

To the extent that's possible, the best strategy is to plan for change and recognize the necessity to accommodate it. With change will come frustrations and discouragements, but also opportunities for those who are alert for them.

Acknowledgments

I gratefully acknowledge the many helpful contributors to the Amazon seller discussions and the eBay booksellers board and also Jerry Zyskowsi of Seattle SCORE (Service Corps of Retired Executives), who provided extremely helpful business advice. I also acknowledge New Zealand mystery author Ngaio Marsh's advice on writing in her unpublished "Letter to a Young Man" and thank my sister Ollie Young for calling my attention to Malcolm Gladwell's intriguing book *Blink*.

References

Anderson, Chris. 2006. *The Long Tail: Why the Future of Business Is Selling Less of More.* Hyperion. 256 pp. ISBN 1615511857.

Friedman, Thomas L. 2005. *The World Is Flat: A Brief History of the Twenty-First Century.* New York: Farrar, Straus, and Giroux. 488 pp. ISBN 0-374-29288-4.

Gates, Bill. 1995. *The Road Ahead.* Viking Press. 304 pp. ISBN 978-0670859139.

Gladwell, Malcolm. 2005. *Blink.* New York: Little, Brown, and Co. 296 pp. ISBN 0-316-01006.

Grove, Andrew. 1996. *Only the Paranoid Survive.* Harper-Collins Business. 210 pp. ISBN 0002558106.

Landahl, John. 2006. *Estate Sale Prospecting for Fun and Profit with craigslist and eBay.* InfoStrategist.com. ISBN 1-59243-287-5.

– -. 2008. *Some Ugly Ducklings Amongst Used Books, 2007.* InfoStrategist.com ebook.

Mould, Michael. 2006. *Online Bookselling: A Practical Guide with Detailed Explanations and Insightful Tips.* Lulu.com. 228 pp. ISBN 1430300493.

Negroponte, Nicolas. 1995. *Being Digital.* Knopf. 256 pp. ISBN 0-679-43919-6.

Weber, Steve. 2005. *The Home-Based Bookstore: Start Your Own Business Selling Used Books on Amazon, eBay or Your Own Web Site.* Weber Books. ISBN 0-9772406-0-6

Windwalker, Stephen. 2002. *Selling Used Books Online.* Harvard Perspective Press. 176 pp. ISBN 0971577838.

Index

Made in the USA
Monee, IL
08 November 2026

67377462R00080